PARTY TREATS

FRIGHTFUL HALLOWEEN TREATS 2

MEXICAN FIESTA 22

HAPPY BIRTHDAY 34

BEACH PARTY.................................52

ICE CREAM SOCIAL 72

Frightful Halloween Treats

HAUNTED HOUSE CUPCAKES

> **1 package (about 19¹/₂ ounces) brownie mix, plus
>   ingredients to prepare mix**
> **10 waffle ice cream bowls**
> **1 container (16 ounces) chocolate or caramel frosting**
> **20 graham crackers**
> **Licorice pieces, chow mein noodles, candy corn, candy
>   pumpkins and other assorted candies**
> **Black decorating gel**

1. Preheat oven to 350°F. Prepare brownie mix according to package directions. Place waffle bowls on baking sheet. Fill waffle bowls about two-thirds full with brownie batter. Bake 25 minutes or until toothpicks inserted into centers come out clean. Cool completely on wire racks.

2. Spread frosting on cooled cupcakes. For each house, break 1 graham cracker into 4 rectangles. Press rectangles into center of cupcake vertically for walls. Cut another rectangle in half; attach to top with frosting for roof. Attach candies to roof with frosting for chimney. Decorate as desired with candies and decorating gel.

Makes 10 servings

2

Haunted House Cupcakes

GUSHING GOO ROLLS

12 soft corn tortillas
2 tablespoons extra virgin olive oil
1 envelope (1¼ ounces) taco seasoning mix
12 mozzarella-cheddar swirled cheese sticks
Nonstick cooking spray

1. Preheat oven to 475 °F.

2. Place one tortilla on ungreased baking sheet. Brush one side of tortilla with oil; sprinkle with 1 teaspoon taco seasoning. Top with one cheese stick; roll-up tightly. Lay seam side down on prepared baking sheet. Repeat with remaining tortillas, seasoning and cheese. Spray tortillas with cooking spray.

3. Bake tortillas 6 minutes or until cheese begins to melt.

4. Remove from oven and let stand 3 minutes to allow cheese to set slightly. *Makes 12 rolls*

Tip: Before assembling rolls, warm tortillas briefly over a burner or in the oven to make them more pliable.

TOMBSTONES

- ¾ **cup all-purpose flour**
- 3 **tablespoons powdered sugar**
- 2 **tablespoons unsweetened cocoa powder**
- ¼ **teaspoon salt**
- 1 **cup water**
- ½ **cup (1 stick) butter, cut into pieces**
- 4 **eggs**
- 1 **package (4-serving size) instant vanilla or white chocolate pudding and pie filling mix**
- ¾ **cup cold milk**
  Orange food coloring
- 1 **container (8 ounces) frozen nondairy whipped topping, thawed**
  Icings and Halloween decors

1. Combine flour, sugar, cocoa and salt in small bowl. Bring water and butter to a boil in medium saucepan over high heat, stirring until butter is melted. Reduce heat to low; add flour mixture. Stir until mixture forms ball. Remove from heat. Add eggs, one at a time, beating after each addition until mixture is smooth.

2. Preheat oven to 375°F. Lightly grease baking sheet. Spoon about ¼ cup dough onto prepared baking sheet. With wet knife, form into tombstone shape, about 3½×2-inches. Repeat with remaining dough to form 10 tombstones, placing about 2 inches apart.

3. Bake 25 to 30 minutes or until puffed and dry on top. Remove to wire racks; cool completely.

4. Meanwhile, combine pudding mix and cold milk in medium bowl until smooth; stir in food coloring. Cover and refrigerate about 20 minutes or until set. Stir whipped topping into pudding until well blended. Cover and refrigerate about 20 minutes or until set.

5. With serrated knife, carefully cut each tombstone in half horizontally; remove soft interior, leaving hollow shell. Decorate top of each shell with icing and decors as desired. Just before serving, fill bottom shells evenly with pudding mixture; cover with top shells.

Makes 10 servings

MONSTROUS MAC & CHEESE

2 packages (7 ounces each) macaroni and cheese mix, plus
ingredients to prepare mix
4 slices pepperoni
Pimiento-stuffed green olives
Ripe black olives
Red, green and/or yellow bell peppers

1. Prepare macaroni and cheese according to package directions.
Transfer to four shallow bowls.

2. Cut pepperoni, olives and peppers into strips and shapes. Arrange
over macaroni for monster faces.   *Makes 4 servings*

GHOST ON A STICK

4 wooden craft sticks
4 medium pears, stems removed
9 squares (2 ounces each) almond bark
Mini chocolate chips

1. Line baking sheet with waxed paper and 4 paper baking cups.
Insert wooden sticks into stem ends of pears.

2. Melt almond bark according to package directions.

3. Dip one pear into melted almond bark, spooning bark over top to
coat evenly. Remove excess by scraping pear bottom across rim of
measuring cup. Place on paper baking cup; let set 1 minute.

4. Decorate with mini chocolate chips to make ghost face. Repeat
with remaining pears. Place spoonful of extra almond bark at bottom
of pears for ghost tails. Refrigerate until firm.   *Makes 4 servings*

Monstrous Mac & Cheese

NIGHT CRAWLER VEGGIE ROLLS

- ¼ cup sesame oil
- 1 teaspoon freshly grated ginger
- 1 teaspoon minced garlic
- 2 large carrots, shredded
- 1 red bell pepper, cut into matchstick-size pieces
- 1 onion, cut into matchstick-size pieces
- ¼ pound snow peas, cut into matchstick-size pieces
- 2 cups bean sprouts
- 2 to 3 cups shredded Napa cabbage
- 1 teaspoon salt
- 1 teaspoon black pepper
- 1 package (12 ounces) spring roll wrappers*
  Sweet and sour sauce (optional)
  Peanut sauce (optional)

Rice paper spring roll wrappers can be found in Asian food sections of most supermarkets.

1. Heat oil, ginger and garlic in wok or large skillet over medium heat. Add carrots, bell pepper, onion and snow peas; stir-fry 2 minutes. Add bean sprouts, cabbage, salt and black pepper; stir-fry 2 more minutes. Remove from heat and cool.

2. Dip spring roll wrappers in hot water until soft. Position wrapper with one point facing down. Place about 2 tablespoons vegetable mixture in narrow strip across lower half of wrapper. Fold bottom point up and over vegetables and tuck behind filling. Roll packet up once to enclose filling securely. Fold sides in tightly, forming an envelope. Finish rolling and brush with additional hot water to seal. For creature features, cut tiny eyes and mouths in wrappers and add vegetable strips for antennae. Repeat with remaining filling and wrappers. Cover with plastic wrap and refrigerate. Serve chilled with dipping sauces, if desired. *Makes 18 to 20 pieces*

PUTRID BUG POTION

3 cups lime sherbet
1 cup pineapple juice
1 package (0.13-ounce) grape-flavored drink mix
2 cups ginger ale
Frozen seedless red grapes (optional)

1. Combine sherbet, juice and drink mix in blender container. Process until smooth.

2. Add ginger ale. Cover; process until just blended.

3. Add frozen grapes, if desired. Serve immediately.

Makes 5 cups

Tip: Fake ice cubes with bugs or other critters can be added for an extra-buggy presentation. Make this grayish, ghoulish concoction pale pink by substituting cherry-flavor drink mix for the grape.

CHEESY SNAILS

1 package (12 ounces) refrigerated French bread dough
5 part-skim mozzarella string cheese sticks
1 egg
1 tablespoon heavy cream
2 tablespoons sesame seeds

1. Preheat oven to 350°F. Line baking sheet with parchment paper. Roll out bread dough into 10×12-inch rectangle; cut in half lengthwise to make 2 (10×6 inch) sheets. Cut each sheet into 5 (2×6-inch) rectangles. Slice cheese sticks in half lengthwise. Crimp piece of dough around each piece of cheese, leaving ¼ inch of cheese exposed at end. Beginning with other end, roll into coil shape to make snail. Place on prepared baking sheet.

2. Beat egg and cream in small bowl. Brush dough coils with egg mixture and sprinkle with sesame seeds. Bake 20 to 25 minutes or until dough is browned and cheese oozes. Cool slightly before serving.

Makes 10 servings

STICKY RICE COFFINS

1 cup uncooked sushi or short-grain rice
1½ cups water
3 tablespoons rice vinegar
1½ tablespoons sugar
⅛ teaspoon salt
1 tablespoon vegetable oil
1 small red onion, finely chopped
1 clove garlic, minced
1 bag (8 ounces) cooked peeled baby shrimp, thawed and drained
1 tablespoon minced fresh cilantro (optional)
1 tablespoon curry powder or Thai green curry paste (optional)
1 cup coconut milk (optional)

1. Combine rice and water in medium saucepan. Bring to a boil. Reduce heat to low; cover and cook 15 minutes or until liquid is absorbed. Set aside 10 minutes.

2. Combine vinegar, sugar and salt in small microwavable bowl. Microwave on HIGH 30 seconds or until sugar dissolves and liquid is hot. Slowly pour vinegar mixture over rice, stirring until liquid is absorbed and rice is sticky. (It may not be necessary to add all vinegar mixture.) Set aside to cool.

3. Heat oil in medium skillet. Add onion and garlic; cook and stir 2 minutes. Add shrimp and cook 2 minutes. Stir shrimp mixture into rice. Stir in cilantro, if desired.

4. Scoop rice mixture into ⅓-cup measuring cup or small mold. Pack down. Turn out onto serving plate. Use a wet spatula to press rice into coffin shape. If desired, combine coconut milk and curry powder in small bowl. Drizzle over rice or serve as dipping sauce.

Makes 10 servings

Sticky Rice Coffin

GHOSTS AT THE WATERING HOLE

1 package (12 ounces) chocolate chips
½ cup whipping cream
2 tablespoons light corn syrup
1 tablespoon butter
Pinch salt
Marshmallows

1. Combine chocolate chips, cream, corn syrup, butter and salt in small saucepan. Heat over low heat until chips melt and mixture is smooth. Pour into fondue pot; set over low heat.

2. Place marshmallows in serving bowl. Set out stack of dessert plates and fondue forks for dipping.   *Makes about 2 cups (12 servings)*

BRIDE OF FRANKENSTEIN TREATS

1 can (6½ ounces) green decorating icing with
   decorator tips
12 prepared crisp rice cereal treats
12 black jelly beans
12 small red licorice strips
24 green jelly beans

1. Pipe stripes of icing across short end of crispy rice treat to create hair.

2. Cut black jelly beans in half; attach to treat using small amount of icing to create eyes. Attach one licorice strip using small amount of icing to create mouth. Attach one green jelly bean using small amount of icing to each side of one treat to create bolts. Repeat with remaining ingredients.   *Makes 12 servings*

SNAKE CALZONES

2 loaves (16 ounces each) frozen white bread dough, thawed
4 tablespoons deli-style mustard, divided
2 tablespoons sun-dried tomato pesto, divided
2 teaspoons Italian seasoning, divided
10 ounces thinly sliced ham, divided
10 ounces thinly sliced salami, divided
1½ cups (6 ounces) provolone cheese, shredded, divided
1½ cups (6 ounces) mozzarella cheese, shredded, divided
2 egg yolks, divided
2 teaspoons water, divided
Red and yellow liquid food coloring

1. Line 2 baking sheets with parchment paper; spray with nonstick cooking spray. Roll out 1 loaf of dough into 24×6-inch rectangle on lightly floured work surface. Spread 2 tablespoons mustard and 1 tablespoon pesto over dough, leaving a 1-inch border; sprinkle with 1 teaspoon Italian seasoning.

2. Layer half of ham and salami over dough. Sprinkle ¾ cup of each cheese over meats. Brush edges of dough with water. Beginning at long side, tightly roll up dough into spiral. Pinch edges to seal. Transfer dough to prepared baking sheet, seam side down; shape into S-shaped snake or coiled snake (leave 1 end unattached to form head on coil). Repeat with remaining ingredients.

3. Combine 1 egg yolk, 1 teaspoon water and red food coloring in small bowl. Combine remaining egg yolk, remaining teaspoon water and yellow food coloring in another small bowl. Paint stripes, dots and zigzags over dough to make snakeskin pattern.

4. Preheat oven to 375°F. Let dough rise, uncovered, in warm place 30 minutes. (Let rise 40 minutes if using a coil shape.) After rising, taper one end of each roll to form head and one end to form tail. Score tail end to form rattlers, if desired.

5. Bake snakes 25 to 30 minutes, slightly longer for coiled snake. Cool slightly. Slice and serve warm. *Makes 24 to 28 servings*

Snake Calzones

20

Mexican Fiesta

TACO TWO-ZIES

- **1 pound ground beef**
- **2 packages (1 ounce each) LAWRY'S® Taco Spices & Seasonings**
- **⅔ cup water**
- **1 can (1 pound 14 ounces) refried beans, warmed**
- **10 small flour tortillas (fajita size), warmed to soften**
- **10 jumbo size taco shells, heated according to package directions**

Taco Toppings
Shredded lettuce, shredded Cheddar cheese and chopped tomatoes

In large skillet, brown ground beef over medium high heat until crumbly; drain fat. Stir in 1 package Taco Spices & Seasonings and water. Bring to a boil; reduce heat to low and cook, uncovered, 10 minutes, stirring occasionally. In medium bowl, mix together beans and remaining package Taco Spices & Seasonings. Spread about ⅓-cup seasoned beans all the way to edges of each flour tortilla. Place a taco shell on center of each bean-tortilla and fold edges up around shell, lightly pressing to 'stick' tortilla to shell. Fill each taco with about 3 tablespoons taco meat. Top with your choice of taco toppings.

Makes 10 tacos

Variations: May use lean ground turkey, chicken or pork in place of ground beef. May use LAWRY'S® Chicken Taco Spices & Seasonings or LAWRY'S® Hot Taco Spices & Seasonings instead of Taco Spices & Seasonings.

Prep. Time: 8 to 10 minutes
Cook Time: 15 minutes

KIDDY QUESADILLAS

**1 can (15 ounces) VEG · ALL® Original Mixed Vegetables,
   drained**
1 pound ground beef, cooked and drained
2 cups shredded taco cheese
½ cup mild salsa
   Salt & pepper to taste
10 teaspoons vegetable oil, divided
10 (6-inch) flour tortillas

Combine the first 5 ingredients in a medium size bowl.

Heat 1 teaspoon of oil in a 10- or 12-inch nonstick skillet over
medium heat. Spread ½ cup of beef mixture onto half of 1 tortilla.
Carefully transfer to hot skillet.

Cook for 1½ to 2 minutes or until golden brown. Fold over one side
with a spatula. Cook an additional 30 to 45 seconds.

Remove from skillet, cut in half and serve. Repeat with remaining
filling and tortillas, if desired, or refrigerate until needed.

Makes 10 quesadillas

MINI NACHO PIZZA

1 sandwich-size English muffin, split, toasted
½ cup refried beans, divided
**2 tablespoons CONTADINA® Pizza Squeeze Pizza Sauce,
   divided**
½ cup (2 ounces) shredded Cheddar cheese, divided
2 tablespoons diced green chiles, drained (optional)

1. Spread each muffin half with ¼ cup refried beans and
1 tablespoon pizza sauce; sprinkle with ¼ cup cheese.

2. Bake in preheated 400°F oven for 10 minutes or until cheese is
melted. Sprinkle with chiles, if desired. *Makes 2 servings*

Prep Time: 5 minutes
Cook Time: 10 minutes

Kiddy Quesadillas

EASY TACO PIZZA

   ½ **pound ground pork**
   2 **tablespoons taco seasoning (½ package)**
   1 **(6½-ounce) package pizza crust mix**
   1 **cup salsa**
   1 **cup reduced-fat shredded Colby Jack cheese**
  ⅔ **cup coarsely crushed tortilla chips**
1½ **cups shredded lettuce**
   2 **tablespoons sliced ripe olives**

Heat oven to 400°F. In large nonstick skillet, cook ground pork with taco seasoning mix over medium heat for about 10 minutes or until pork is crumbly and no longer pink. Prepare pizza crust according to package directions. Spread crust evenly on greased 12-inch pizza pan and top evenly with salsa. Sprinkle with pork mixture, cheese and tortilla chips. Bake for 18 to 22 minutes or until crust is golden brown. Remove from oven; top with shredded lettuce and olives.

Makes 6 servings

Favorite recipe from **National Pork Board**

TACO TATERS

   1 **pound ground beef**
   1 **jar (1 pound 10 ounces) RAGÚ® Old World Style® Pasta Sauce**
   1 **package (1.25 ounces) taco seasoning mix**
   6 **large all-purpose potatoes, unpeeled and baked**

1. In 12-inch skillet, brown ground beef over medium-high heat; drain. Stir in Ragú Pasta Sauce and taco seasoning mix and cook 5 minutes.

2. To serve, cut a lengthwise slice from top of each potato. Evenly spoon beef mixture onto each potato. Garnish, if desired, with shredded Cheddar cheese and sour cream.

Makes 6 servings

Prep Time: 5 minutes
Cook Time: 15 minutes

DULCE DE LECHE DESSERT SANDWICHES

1 pint (2 cups) Dulce de Leche ice cream
¾ cup pecans
12 chocolate cookies

1. Preheat oven to 350°F.

2. Remove ice cream from freezer; let stand at room temperature 10 minutes or until slightly softened.

3. Place pecans in single layer in shallow baking pan. Bake 8 minutes or until golden and fragrant; set aside to cool. Finely chop pecans; reserve.

4. Spread ⅓ cup ice cream onto flat sides of 6 cookies. Place remaining cookies, flat sides down, on ice cream; press cookies together lightly. Smooth edges; remove excess ice cream, if necessary. Wrap each sandwich individually in plastic wrap; freeze 30 minutes or until firm.

5. Press pecans into ice cream around edges; rewrap in plastic. Freeze additional 30 minutes.   *Makes 6 servings*

Note: Ice cream sandwiches should be eaten within three days. After three days, cookies will absorb moisture and become soggy.

CHOCOLATE FLAN

2 eggs, lightly beaten
24 packets NatraTaste® Brand Sugar Substitute
2 heaping tablespoons unsweetened cocoa powder
1 tablespoon cornstarch
1 teaspoon almond extract
1 (15-ounce) can evaporated skim milk
1 cup fat-free milk

1. Preheat oven to 350°F. Coat a 3-cup mold with nonstick cooking spray.

2. In a medium bowl, whisk together eggs, NatraTaste®, cocoa, cornstarch and almond extract until smooth. Stir in evaporated milk and fat-free milk. Pour mixture into mold. Place mold in a baking pan filled halfway with water.*

3. Bake 2 hours. Mixture will not look completely set, but will become firm upon cooling. Let cool at room temperature 1 hour, then refrigerate for several hours. To serve, invert mold onto a plate, or spoon flan from the mold.   *Makes 8 servings*

Placing baking mold in water helps cook the flan evenly without cracking.

Tip: Flan is a traditional dessert served in Mexico and Spain. This version is a creative change from the typical caramel flavor.

CREAMY DREAMY TACO TREATS

¼ **cup plus 2 tablespoons packed light brown sugar**
2 **egg whites**
2 **tablespoons butter, melted and slightly cooled**
1 **teaspoon vanilla**
½ **teaspoon ground cinnamon**
¼ **teaspoon ground nutmeg**
½ **cup pecans or walnuts, chopped**
2 **tablespoons all-purpose flour**
2⅔ **cups vanilla or chocolate ice cream**
   Fresh chopped strawberries and pineapple
   Chocolate sprinkles

1. Preheat oven to 375°F.

2. Beat sugar, egg whites, butter, vanilla, cinnamon and nutmeg in medium bowl with electric mixer at medium speed 1 minute.

3. Combine pecans and flour in work bowl of food processor. Pulse until coarsely ground. Add to sugar mixture and stir until well blended. Let stand 10 minutes to thicken.

4. Spray baking sheet with nonstick cooking spray. Spoon 2 tablespoons batter onto sheet. Using back of spoon, spread into 5-inch diameter circle. Repeat with another 2 tablespoons batter, placed 4 to 5 inches apart. Bake 5 minutes or until light brown. Cool on wire rack 1 minute. Gently remove each cookie with metal spatula and place over rolling pin. Let cool 5 minutes. Repeat with remaining batter.

5. Fill each cookie with ⅓ cup ice cream. Wrap in plastic wrap; freeze until ready to serve. Top with fruit and chocolate sprinkles before serving. *Makes 6 treats*

Creamy Dreamy Taco Treat

DESSERT NACHOS

    3 (6- to 7-inch) flour tortillas
      Nonstick cooking spray
    1 tablespoon sugar
   ⅛ teaspoon ground cinnamon
      Dash ground allspice
    1 container (6 to 8 ounces) vanilla yogurt
    1 teaspoon grated orange peel
  1½ cups strawberries
   ½ cup blueberries
    4 teaspoons miniature semisweet chocolate chips

1. Preheat oven to 375°F.

2. Cut each tortilla into 8 wedges. Place on ungreased baking sheet. Generously spray tortilla wedges with cooking spray. Combine sugar, cinnamon and allspice in small bowl. Sprinkle sugar mixture over tortilla wedges. Bake 7 to 9 minutes or until lightly browned; cool completely.

3. Meanwhile, combine yogurt and orange peel. Stem strawberries; cut lengthwise into quarters.

4. Place 6 tortilla wedges on each of 4 small plates. Top with strawberries and blueberries. Drizzle with yogurt mixture. Sprinkle with chocolate chips. Serve immediately. *Makes 4 servings*

Dessert Nachos

Happy Birthday

HAPPY CLOWN FACE

**1 package (18¼ ounces) white cake mix, plus ingredients
    to prepare mix**
1 container (16 ounces) white frosting
Food coloring
**Assorted gum drops, gummy candies, colored licorice
    strings and other candies**
1 party hat
Candles

1. Prepare and bake cake according to package directions for two
8- or 9-inch round cakes. Cool cake layers completely before frosting.

2. Combine frosting and food coloring in medium bowl until desired
shade is reached. Place one cake layer on serving plate; spread top
with frosting. Top with second cake layer; frost top and side of cake.

3. Decorate face of clown using assorted candies. Arrange party hat
and candles on cake as desired.   *Makes 12 servings*

Happy Clown Face

COOKIE PIZZA CAKE

1 package (18 ounces) refrigerated chocolate chip cookie dough
1 package (18¼ ounces) chocolate cake mix, plus ingredients to prepare mix
1 cup prepared vanilla frosting
½ cup peanut butter
1 to 2 tablespoons milk
1 container (16 ounces) chocolate frosting
Chocolate peanut butter cups, chopped (optional)

1. Preheat oven to 350°F. Coat two 12×1-inch round pizza pans with nonstick cooking spray. Press cookie dough evenly into one pan. Bake 15 to 20 minutes or until edges are golden brown. Cool 20 minutes in pan on wire rack. Remove from pan; cool completely on wire rack.

2. Prepare cake mix according to package directions. Fill second pan ¼ to ½ full with batter. (Reserve remaining cake batter for another use, such as cupcakes.) Bake 10 to 15 minutes or until toothpick inserted into center comes out clean. Cool 15 minutes on wire rack. Gently remove cake from pan; cool completely.

3. Combine vanilla frosting and peanut butter in small bowl. Gradually stir in milk, 1 tablespoon at a time, until mixture is of spreadable consistency.

4. Place cookie on serving plate. Spread peanut butter frosting over cookie. Place cake on top of cookie, trimming cookie to match the size of cake, if necessary. Frost top and side of cake with chocolate frosting. Garnish with peanut butter cups, if desired.

Makes 12 to 14 servings

LOLLIPOP GARDEN BOUQUET

**1 package (18¼ ounces) carrot cake mix, plus ingredients
    to prepare mix**
1 container (16 ounces) white frosting
    Green food coloring
½ cup crushed chocolate wafer cookies
    Round hard sweet and sour candies
20 hard candy rings
    Green fruit leather
6 to 10 lollipops

1. Prepare and bake cake mix according to package directions for one 8-inch round cake and one 9-inch round cake. Cool completely before frosting.

2. Combine frosting and food coloring in medium bowl until desired shade is reached. Place 8-inch cake layer on serving plate; spread top and side with frosting. Top with 9-inch cake layer; frost top and side of cake.

3. Sprinkle top of cake with cookie crumbs, leaving 1-inch border around edge of cake. Arrange round candies around top edge of cake as shown in photo. Press candy rings into side of bottom cake layer.

4. Use scissors to cut fruit leather into 2½-inch leaf shapes. Press leaves onto lollipop sticks; arrange lollipops in center of cake.

Makes 12 servings

38

Lollipop Garden Bouquet

COOKIE SUNDAE CUPS

1 package (18 ounces) refrigerated chocolate chip cookie dough
6 cups ice cream, any flavor
Ice cream topping, any flavor
Whipped cream
Colored sprinkles

1. Preheat oven to 350°F. Lightly grease 18 standard (2½-inch) muffin pan cups.

2. Remove dough from wrapper. Shape dough into 18 balls; press onto bottoms and up sides of prepared muffin cups.

3. Bake 14 to 18 minutes or until golden brown. Cool in pans 10 minutes. Remove to wire rack; cool completely.

4. Place ⅓ cup ice cream in each cookie cup. Drizzle with ice cream topping. Top with whipped cream and colored sprinkles.

Makes 1½ dozen cups

Cookie Sundae Cup

FUNNY FACE FRUIT PIZZAS

3 tablespoons sugar
1 teaspoon ground cinnamon
6 (6-inch) flour tortillas
2 tablespoons water
1 package (1 ounce) instant sugar-free vanilla pudding (4 servings)
1 DOLE® Banana, sliced
½ DOLE® Mango, peeled, sliced
1 DOLE® Kiwi fruit, peeled, sliced
   DOLE® Seedless Raisins (optional)
   DOLE® Strawberries (optional)

- Combine sugar and cinnamon. Brush tortillas lightly with water. Sprinkle sugar mixture on top of tortillas.

- Place tortillas on baking sheet sprayed with vegetable cooking spray. Bake at 400°F 10 minutes or until lightly browned.

- Prepare pudding according to package directions.

- Spoon about ⅓ cup pudding onto each tortilla. Arrange banana, mango, kiwi, raisins and strawberries on pudding to make a funny face or design. Serve. *Makes 6 servings*

Prep Time: 10 minutes
Bake Time: 10 minutes

42

BIRTHDAY CAKE COOKIES

1 package (18 ounces) refrigerated sugar cookie dough
1 container (16 ounces) prepared white frosting
   Food coloring (optional)
   Colored sprinkles or decors
10 small birthday candles

1. Preheat oven to 350°F. Lightly grease 10 mini (1¾-inch) muffin pan cups and 10 standard (2½-inch) muffin pan cups. Shape one-third of dough into 10 (1-inch) balls; press onto bottoms and up sides of prepared mini muffin cups. Shape remaining two-thirds of dough into 10 equal balls; press onto bottoms and up sides of prepared standard muffin cups.

2. Bake mini cookies 8 to 9 minutes or until edges are light brown. Bake regular cookies 10 to 11 minutes or until edges are light brown. Cool 5 minutes in pans on wire racks. Remove cookies to wire racks; cool completely.

3. Add food coloring, if desired, to frosting; mix well. Spread frosting over top and side of each cookie. Place 1 mini cookie on top of 1 regular cookie. Decorate with sprinkles. Press 1 candle into center of each cookie.   *Makes 10 cookie cakes*

SURPRISE PACKAGE CUPCAKES

 1 **package (18¼ ounces) chocolate cake mix, plus**
   ingredients to prepare mix
   Food coloring (optional)
 1 **container (16 ounces) vanilla frosting**
 1 **tube (4¼ ounces) white decorating icing**
72 **chewy fruit squares**
   Colored decors and birthday candles (optional)

1. Line 24 standard (2½-inch) muffin pan cups with paper liners or spray with nonstick cooking spray. Prepare and bake cake mix in prepared muffin cups according to package directions. Cool in pans on wire racks 15 minutes. Remove cupcakes to racks; cool completely.

2. If desired, tint frosting with food coloring, adding a few drops at a time until desired color is reached. Spread frosting over cupcakes.

3. Use decorating icing to pipe "ribbons" on fruit squares to resemble wrapped presents. Place 3 candy presents on each cupcake. Decorate with decors and candles, if desired. *Makes 24 cupcakes*

THE SWEET EXPRESS

1 package (18¼ ounces) marble cake mix, plus ingredients to prepare mix
1 container (16 ounces) vanilla frosting
Blue decorating spray
Decorating icing, any 3 colors
½ cup chopped nuts or crushed cinnamon graham cracker crumbs
7 mini chocolate sandwich cookies
Sugar-coated sour gummy strips, any colors
Gummy candy rings
Assorted small candies

1. Preheat oven to 350°F. Grease and flour 13×9-inch cake pan. Prepare cake mix according to package directions.

2. Bake 32 to 35 minutes or until toothpick inserted into center comes out clean. Cool cake in pan about 20 minutes; remove from pan and cool completely on wire rack.

3. Place cake on serving platter; frost top and sides with frosting. Spray top third of cake with blue decorating spray to resemble clouds. Using toothpick, draw outline for train cars. Following outline, frost each train car with desired icing color. Sprinkle chopped nuts under train cars. Place sandwich cookies on train cars to resemble wheels.

4. Cut shapes from gummy strips to resemble car connectors, windows, cowcatcher and smoke stack; arrange on train as shown in photo. Arrange gummy candy rings to resemble smoke rings. Decorate train cars and edge of cake with assorted candies as desired.

Makes 12 servings

TRIPLE CHOCOLATE CUPS

2 cups low-fat chocolate frozen yogurt
1 cup fat-free (skim) milk
2 tablespoons chocolate syrup
¼ cup crushed chocolate wafer crumbs
   Whipped cream or nondairy topping
   Chocolate sprinkles or decors (optional)

1. Line 24 mini (1¾-inch) muffin pan cups with paper liners. Combine yogurt, milk and chocolate syrup in blender; cover. Blend on HIGH speed until smooth. Add chocolate wafer crumbs; cover and pulse on HIGH speed until mixed. Spoon mixture into prepared muffin cups, filling three-fourths full. Freeze 1 hour or until solid.

2. If liners stick to muffin pan, thaw at room temperature 10 to 15 minutes or until liners can be easily removed. Just before serving, garnish with whipped cream and chocolate sprinkles. Freeze leftovers in airtight container. *Makes 24 cups*

Tip: Have your child help by filling the muffin liners or adding the sprinkles.

RAINBOW CAKES

**1 package (18¼ ounces) cake mix (any flavor), plus
   ingredients to prepare mix**
⅓ cup raspberry jam
**1 container (16 ounces) vanilla frosting
   Multi-colored coated fruit candies**

1. Prepare cake mix and bake in 17×11-inch jelly-roll pan according to package directions. Remove from oven; cool completely in pan on wire rack.

2. Using knife or square cookie cutter, cut 15 (2½-inch) squares from cake. Spread raspberry jam on one cake layer; top with second layer. Spread with jam and top with third cake layer.

3. Frost entire cake with vanilla frosting. Repeat to make 5 cakes. Sprinkle with candies or decorate as desired.   *Makes 5 cakes*

Note: For easy icing application, first brush the crumbs from the cake layers. Then apply a very thin "crumb coating" of icing on the cake. Place the cake in the freezer for about 20 minutes, then apply the second, decorative frosting layer to the top and sides of the cake.

Rainbow Cake

Beach Party

BOATS IN THE OCEAN

3 large zucchini, halved lengthwise
1 tablespoon water
1 tablespoon olive oil
1 jar (2 pounds) RAGÚ® Rich & Meaty Meat Sauce
8 ounces mafalde or other long wavy pasta, cooked and drained
1 cup shredded mozzarella cheese (about 4 ounces)

Scoop pulp from zucchini; set aside. In 11×7-inch microwave-safe baking dish, arrange zucchini halves. Add water, cover with plastic wrap and microwave at HIGH 5 minutes or until tender; set aside.

Meanwhile, chop zucchini pulp. In 10-inch nonstick skillet, heat olive oil over medium-high heat and cook zucchini pulp, stirring occasionally, 5 minutes or until golden. Stir in Meat Sauce and simmer 3 minutes.

To serve, arrange hot pasta on blue serving plate. Arrange zucchini boats on pasta, cut-side up, then fill each boat with sauce mixture. Sprinkle boats with cheese and serve immediately. Decorate, if desired, with homemade or purchased "sails."   *Makes 6 servings*

Prep Time: 20 minutes
Cook Time: 11 minutes

MINI PICKLE SEA MONSTER BURGERS

4 large hamburger buns
2 whole dill pickles
1 pound 95% lean ground beef
2 tablespoons steak sauce
  Salt and black pepper
3 American cheese slices, cut into 4 squares each
  Ketchup

1. Preheat broiler.

2. Cut 3 circles out of each bun half with 2-inch biscuit cutter; set aside. Discard scraps.

3. Slice pickles lengthwise into thin slices. Using 12 largest slices, cut 4 to 5 slits on one end of each slice, about ½ inch deep; fan slightly to resemble fish tails. Set aside. Save remaining slices for another use.

4. Spray broiler rack and pan with nonstick cooking spray; set aside.

5. Combine ground beef and steak sauce in medium bowl; mix until just blended. Shape meat into 12 (2½ × ¼-inch) patties. Place on broiler rack. Sprinkle with salt and pepper. Broil 4 inches from heat 2 minutes. Turn patties and broil 2 minutes longer or until no longer pink in center. Remove from heat; top with cheese squares.

6. Arrange bun bottoms on serving platter; top with ketchup and pickle slices, making sure slices stick out at both ends. Place cheeseburgers on top of pickles; top with bun tops. Place drop of ketchup on uncut end of pickle to resemble eye.

Makes 12 mini burgers

Mini Pickle Sea Monster Burgers

FISH BITERS

24 giant goldfish-shaped crackers
12 slices pepperoni, halved
12 Monterey Jack cheese cubes, halved
24 small olive slices
24 flat leaf parsley leaves

1. Preheat oven to 425°F

2. Coat large baking sheet with nonstick cooking spray.

3. Place crackers on prepared baking sheet and place two pepperoni halves on each tail end. Place cheese half in center of each fish.

4. Bake 3 minutes or until cheese is melted. Remove from oven and immediately top with olive slice to resemble eye.

5. Lift up olive slice slightly and place a parsley leaf behind it to resemble fin. Gently press down on olive to adhere. Serve warm.

Makes 24 crackers

Tip: Fish may be assembled up to 2 hours in advance. Complete steps 1 and 2, then cover with a sheet of plastic wrap or foil and refrigerate until ready to bake.

CONCH SHELLS

2 tablespoons butter, softened
2 tablespoons packed brown sugar
⅛ teaspoon ground cinnamon
1 can (8 ounces) refrigerated crescent roll dough
½ cup raisins
1 egg white, slightly beaten
   Granulated sugar

1. Preheat oven to 375°F. Combine butter, brown sugar and cinnamon in small bowl; set aside.

2. Unroll crescent roll dough and separate into pre-scored triangles. Cut each triangle into 3 equal size triangles. Spread 1 side of each triangle with about ½ teaspoon butter mixture; sprinkle evenly with raisins. Roll each triangle at a slight angle from the straight-sided base toward the triangular tip in the shape of a conch shell. Place on baking sheet.

3. Brush pastries with egg white and sprinkle with granulated sugar.

4. Bake 8 to 10 minutes until golden brown. Cool on wire rack.

Makes 24 servings

Serving Suggestion: Design your own sea shore! Make sand by combining equal parts finely crushed graham crackers and raw sugar crystals. Spread sand on a large platter and arrange conch shells on top.

TROPICAL PARASOL CAKE

1 package (18¼ ounces) French vanilla cake mix with pudding in the mix, plus ingredients to prepare mix
2 teaspoons coconut extract
1 container (18 ounces) white frosting, divided
¼ cup apricot preserves
2 small bananas, cut into ½-inch slices
  Green food coloring
  Flaked coconut
  Blue food coloring
  Yellow decorating sugar
8 parasols

1. Preheat oven to 350°F. Grease and flour two 9-inch round cake pans.

2. Prepare cake mix according to package directions, stirring coconut extract into batter. Divide batter evenly between prepared pans. Bake 22 minutes or until toothpicks inserted into centers come out clean. Cool completely in pans on wire racks.

3. Combine ½ cup frosting and apricot preserves in small bowl; mix well. Remove cakes from pans. Place one cake layer upside down on serving plate; spread with frosting mixture. Arrange banana slices over frosting; top with second cake layer. Blend remaining frosting and green food coloring in medium bowl until desired shade of green is reached. Frost top and side of cake with green frosting.

4. Place coconut and 8 to 10 drops of blue food coloring in resealable food storage bag; seal bag. Shake bag until coconut is evenly tinted, adding additional food coloring, one drop at a time, until desired shade of blue is reached. Gently press coconut around side of cake. Sprinkle cake with sugar; arrange open parasols around top of cake. *Makes 12 servings*

FISHY SQUISHY SQUIRTERS

20 brightly colored fruit leather rolls
40 seedless red or green grapes, rinsed and patted dry
   Black decorating gel
20 red hot candies

1. Unwrap one piece of fruit leather and place on clean work surface.

2. Arrange 2 grapes, end to end lengthwise, about 1 inch from one corner. Fold nearest corner over grapes; wrap sides in to cover fold and form triangle. Pinch fruit leather together at base of grapes to make tail. Place on waxed paper-lined plate and repeat with remaining grapes and fruit leathers. Shape tails to fan out.

3. Place two large dots of decorating gel on each fish to form base for eyes. Place red hot candy on each dot. Loosely cover with plastic wrap and store in cool dry place until ready to serve.

Makes 20 fish

Tip: For a variation, use mini candy-coated plain chocolate candy pieces instead of red hot candies for fish eyes.

Fishy Squishy Squirters

UNDER THE SEA CAKE

1 package (18¼ ounces) chocolate cake mix, plus
ingredients to prepare mix
1 container (16 ounces) vanilla frosting
Blue food coloring
Assorted sea life gummy candies and rock candy

1. Preheat oven to 350°F. Grease and flour 13×9-inch cake pan.

2. Prepare cake mix according to package directions. Pour batter into prepared pan. Bake 32 to 35 minutes or until toothpick inserted into center comes out clean. Cool cake in pan about 20 minutes; remove from pan and cool completely on wire rack.

3. Blend frosting and food coloring in medium bowl until desired shade of blue is reached. Place cake on serving platter; frost top and sides of cake.

4. Decorate cake with gummy candies and rock candy as desired.

Makes 12 servings

Under the Sea Cake

TROPICAL LUAU CUPCAKES

2 cans (8 ounces each) crushed pineapple in juice
**1 package (18¼ ounces) yellow cake mix *without* pudding
   in the mix**
**1 package (4–serving size) banana cream instant pudding
   and pie filling mix**
4 eggs
⅓ cup vegetable oil
¼ teaspoon ground nutmeg
1 can (12 ounces) whipped vanilla frosting
¾ cup flaked coconut, toasted*
3 to 4 medium kiwi
30 (2½-inch) pretzel sticks

**To toast coconut, spread evenly on ungreased baking sheet; bake in preheated
350°F oven 4 to 6 minutes or until light golden brown, stirring frequently.*

1. Preheat oven to 350°F. Line 30 standard (2½-inch) muffin pan
cups with paper liners. Drain pineapple, reserving juice. Set pineapple
aside.

2. Beat reserved pineapple juice, cake mix, pudding mix, eggs, oil
and nutmeg in large bowl with electric mixer at low speed 1 minute
or until blended. Increase speed to medium; beat 1 to 2 minutes or
until smooth. Fold in pineapple. Fill muffin cups two-thirds full.

3. Bake 20 minutes or until toothpicks inserted into centers come
out clean. Cool cupcakes in pans on wire rack 5 minutes. Remove
from pans; cool completely on wire racks.

4. Frost tops of cupcakes with frosting; sprinkle with coconut. For
palm trees,* peel kiwi and cut into ⅛-inch slices. Create palm fronds
by cutting each slice at ⅜-inch intervals, cutting from outside edge
toward center. (Leave about ¾- to 1-inch circle uncut in center of
each slice). For palm tree trunk, push pretzel stick into, but not
through, center of each kiwi slice. Push other end of pretzel into top
of each cupcake.   *Makes 30 cupcakes*

*Palm tree decorations can be made up to 1 hour before serving.

68

DOLPHIN CAKE

1 **package (18¼ ounces) orange-flavored cake mix, plus ingredients to prepare mix**
1 **container (16 ounces) vanilla frosting, divided**
Yellow food coloring
Blue food coloring
Mini candy-coated chocolate pieces
Silver dragées
Blue sprinkles
Colored sugar and blue rock candy (optional)

1. Prepare and bake cake mix according to package directions for 13×9-inch cake. Cool cake in pan about 20 minutes; remove from pan and cool completely on wire rack.

2. Reserve ¼ cup frosting in small bowl. Blend remaining frosting and yellow food coloring in medium bowl until desired shade of yellow is reached. Place cake on serving platter; frost top and sides of cake with yellow frosting.

3. Draw outline of dolphin in center of cake using toothpick. Blend reserved ¼ cup frosting and blue food coloring in small bowl until desired shade of blue is reached. Spread thin layer of blue frosting within outline of dolphin. Decorate dolphin with chocolate pieces, dragées and sprinkles. Decorate edge and sides of cake with colored sugar and rock candy, if desired.   *Makes 12 servings*

Ice Cream Social

CLOWN-AROUND CONES

4 waffle cones
½ cup "M&M's"® Chocolate Mini Baking Bits, divided
Prepared decorator icing
½ cup hot fudge ice cream topping, divided
4 cups any flavor ice cream, softened
1 (1.5- to 2-ounce) chocolate candy bar, chopped
¼ cup caramel ice cream topping

Decorate cones as desired with "M&M's"® Chocolate Mini Baking Bits, using decorator icing to attach; let set. For each cone, place 1 tablespoon hot fudge topping in bottom of cone. Sprinkle with 1 teaspoon "M&M's"® Chocolate Mini Baking Bits. Layer with ¼ cup ice cream; sprinkle with ¼ of candy bar. Layer with ¼ cup ice cream; sprinkle with 1 teaspoon "M&M's"® Chocolate Mini Baking Bits. Top with 1 tablespoon caramel topping and remaining ½ cup ice cream. Wrap in plastic wrap and freeze until ready to serve. Just before serving, top each ice cream cone with 1 tablespoon hot fudge topping; sprinkle with remaining "M&M's"® Chocolate Mini Baking Bits. Serve immediately. *Makes 4 servings*

FLYING SAUCER ICE CREAM SANDWICHES

1½ pints vanilla ice cream, softened
1 package (9 ounces) chocolate wafer cookies (see Tip)
22 mini chocolate-covered peppermint patties (12 grams each)
Colored candy dots, cinnamon candies, candy-coated chocolate pieces or other candies for decoration

1. Line baking sheet with waxed paper or foil and place in freezer.

2. Scoop 2 tablespoons ice cream onto 1 chocolate wafer. Top with second wafer; press wafers together slightly to push ice cream to edges. Smooth edges. Place on prepared baking sheet in freezer. Repeat with remaining ingredients, making a total of 22 sandwiches. Freeze sandwiches until solid.

3. Decorate sandwiches one at a time. To attach chocolate peppermint patties to tops of each sandwich, heat a table knife over hot stove burner 2 to 3 seconds or until hot. Rub knife on patty until it begins to melt. Lightly press patty, melted side down, to center top of sandwich. Hold until secure. Reheat knife; melt small area on top of chocolate patty; stick piece of candy to melted area and hold until secure. Decorate ice cream edges of sandwich with more candies. Return to freezer. Repeat with remaining sandwiches and candies.

4. Keep frozen until ready to serve.   *Makes 22 servings*

Cook's Tip: If chocolate wafers are unavailable, use chocolate sandwich cookies. Twist cookie to separate cookies from filling. Scrape and discard filling, reserving cookies for ice cream sandwiches.

Flying Saucer Ice Cream Sandwich

PEANUT BUTTER CUP COOKIE ICE CREAM PIE

- ½ **cup creamy peanut butter**
- ¼ **cup honey**
- 1 **quart (2 pints) vanilla ice cream, softened**
- 1 **cup KEEBLER® Chips Deluxe™ With Peanut Butter Cups Cookies, chopped**
- 1 **(6-ounce) READY CRUST® Chocolate Pie Crust**
- ½ **cup chocolate syrup**
  Whipped cream

1. Place large bowl in freezer. Mix peanut butter and honey in medium bowl. Place ice cream in bowl from freezer; add peanut butter mixture and cookies. Mix on low speed with electric mixer until blended.

2. Spoon half of ice cream mixture into crust. Spread chocolate syrup over ice cream mixture layer. Spoon remaining ice cream mixture over chocolate syrup.

3. Garnish with whipped cream and additional chocolate syrup. Freeze leftovers. *Makes 8 servings*

Prep Time: 15 minutes

Peanut Butter Cup Cookie Ice Cream Pie

CARAMEL SUNDAE

1 cup low-fat (1%) milk
1 tablespoon cornstarch
½ cup packed dark brown sugar
1 tablespoon margarine
1 teaspoon vanilla
1 pint vanilla ice milk or fat-free frozen yogurt, divided

1. Combine milk and cornstarch in heavy saucepan. Stir until cornstarch is completely dissolved. Add brown sugar and margarine; cook over medium-low heat, stirring constantly with wire whisk. Bring to a boil. Boil 1 minute. Remove from heat; stir in vanilla. Cool to room temperature.

2. Place ½ cup ice milk in each of four sherbet glasses. Top each with ¼ cup caramel sauce.   *Makes 4 servings*

Tip: Ice milk is made the same way as ice cream, except that it contains less buttermilk and milk solids. The result is a lower calorie count and a lighter texture.

SQUISHED AND SQUIRMY SANDWICHES

1 package (about 9 ounces) vanilla confetti cake mix with pudding in the mix
⅓ cup vegetable oil
2 eggs
1 quart vanilla ice cream
32 gummy worms

1. Preheat oven to 375°F.

2. Combine cake mix, oil and eggs in large bowl. Mix with spoon until well moistened.

3. Shape dough into 32 balls, about 1¼ inches each. Place 2 inches apart on ungreased baking sheets. Gently flatten balls to ¼-inch thickness.

4. Bake 6 to 8 minutes or until edges are lightly golden brown. Cool 1 minute on wire rack. Remove and cool completely.

5. Working quickly, place 2 tablespoons ice cream on flat side of 1 cookie and top with gummy worm, allowing worm to stick out as much as possible. Top with another 2 tablespoons ice cream and another worm. Top with another cookie, flat side down, pressing down to flatten slightly. Wrap in foil and freeze.

6. Repeat with remaining ingredients.   *Makes 16 sandwiches*

STRAWBERRY & CHOCOLATE SHAKE

- ¼ cup sugar
- 3 tablespoons HERSHEY'S Cocoa
- ¼ cup water
- ½ cup cold milk
- 1½ cups sliced fresh strawberries
- 1 teaspoon vanilla extract
- 2 cups (1 pint) vanilla ice cream

Stir together sugar and cocoa in small microwave-safe bowl; stir in water. Microwave at HIGH (100%) 30 to 45 seconds until hot; stir until sugar is dissolved. Cool to room temperature. Place cocoa mixture, milk, strawberries and vanilla in blender container. Cover; blend well. Add ice cream. Cover; blend until smooth. Serve immediately.   *Makes 5 servings*

"MAKE YOUR OWN SUNDAE" PIE

- **1 cup hot fudge ice cream topping, warmed and divided**
- **1 prepared (9-inch) vanilla cookie crumb pie crust**
- **6 cups vanilla ice cream, softened**
- **1 cup caramel ice cream topping, warmed and divided**
- **¼ cup marshmallow cream**
- **1 tablespoon milk**
- **⅔ cup "M&M's"® Chocolate Mini Baking Bits**
- **¼ cup chopped nuts**
- **Aerosol whipped topping and maraschino cherry for garnish**

Spread ½ cup hot fudge topping on bottom of crust; freeze
10 minutes. Spread 1 cup ice cream over fudge layer; freeze
10 minutes. Spread ½ cup caramel topping over ice cream layer;
freeze 10 minutes. Mound scoops of ice cream over caramel layer.
Cover and freeze until ready to serve. Just before serving, in small
bowl combine marshmallow cream and milk. Microwave at HIGH
10 seconds; stir until well combined. Drizzle pie with remaining ½ cup
hot fudge topping, remaining ½ cup caramel topping and
marshmallow sauce. Sprinkle with ⅓ cup "M&M's"® Chocolate Mini
Baking Bits and nuts. Garnish with whipped topping, remaining ⅓ cup
"M&M's"® Chocolate Mini Baking Bits and maraschino cherry. Serve
immediately. *Makes 8 servings*

MICE CREAMS

1 pint vanilla ice cream
**1 (4-ounce) package READY CRUST® Mini-Graham
    Cracker Pie Crusts**
Ears—12 KEEBLER® Grasshopper® cookies
**Tails—3 chocolate twigs, broken in half *or* 6 (3-inch)
    pieces black shoestring licorice**
**Eyes and noses—18 brown candy-coated chocolate
    candies**
Whiskers—2 teaspoons chocolate sprinkles

Place 1 scoop vanilla ice cream into each crust. Press cookie ears and
tails into ice cream. Press eyes, noses and whiskers in place. Serve
immediately. Do not refreeze.   *Makes 6 servings*

Prep Time: 15 minutes

CHOCOLATE ICE CREAM CUPS

2 cups (12 ounces) semisweet chocolate chips
**1 (14-ounce) can EAGLE BRAND® Sweetened Condensed
    Milk (NOT evaporated milk)**
1 cup finely ground pecans
Ice cream, any flavor

1. In heavy saucepan, over low heat, melt chocolate chips with
EAGLE BRAND®; remove from heat. Stir in pecans. In individual
paper-lined muffin cups, spread about 2 tablespoons chocolate
mixture. With lightly greased spoon, spread chocolate on bottom and
up side of each cup.

2. Freeze 2 hours or until firm. Before serving, remove paper liners.
Fill chocolate cups with ice cream. Store unfilled cups tightly covered
in freezer.   *Makes about 1½ dozen cups*

Note: It is easier to remove the paper liners if the chocolate cups sit
at room temperature for about 5 minutes first.

FRUITY DESSERT CUPS

1 can (8 ounces) pineapple chunks in juice, drained
1 ¼ cups seedless red grapes
2 kiwi, peeled and sliced
4 scoops vanilla ice cream

1. Combine fruits; cover. Refrigerate.

2. When ready to serve, spoon fruit mixture into individual dessert
dishes. Top with ice cream. *Makes 4 servings*

MINI MORSEL ICE CREAM PIE

1 ½ cups graham cracker crumbs
½ cup (1 stick) butter, melted
¼ cup granulated sugar
1 cup (6 ounces) NESTLÉ® TOLL HOUSE® Semi-Sweet
   Chocolate Mini Morsels
1 quart ice cream or frozen yogurt, softened

COMBINE graham cracker crumbs, butter and sugar in medium
bowl; stir in morsels. Press *2½ cups* crumb mixture evenly on bottom
and side of 9-inch pie plate. Freeze for 15 minutes or until firm.
Spread softened ice cream evenly in pie shell. Top with *remaining*
crumb mixture; freeze for 2 hours or until firm. *Makes 8 servings*

PEANUT BUSTER BAR DESSERT

2½ cups crushed round chocolate sandwich cookies
  6 tablespoons butter, softened
  2 quarts vanilla ice cream or ice milk, slightly softened
  2 cups powdered sugar
1½ cups evaporated milk
  ⅔ cup semi-sweet chocolate chips
  ½ cup (1 stick) butter
1½ teaspoons WATKINS® Vanilla
1½ cups Spanish peanuts

Mix cookie crumbs and 6 tablespoons softened butter in medium bowl; pat into 13×9-inch baking dish. Chill in freezer until set. Pack ice cream into chocolate crust; return to freezer.

Combine powdered sugar, milk, chocolate chips and ½ cup butter in medium saucepan; bring to a boil over medium heat, stirring constantly, until melted and smooth. Remove from heat and add vanilla; let sauce cool slightly. Sprinkle peanuts over ice cream; top with chocolate sauce. Return to freezer until frozen.

Makes 18 servings

FROZEN BERRY ICE CREAM

- **8 ounces frozen unsweetened strawberries, partially thawed**
- **8 ounces frozen unsweetened peaches, partially thawed**
- **4 ounces frozen unsweetened blueberries, partially thawed**
- **6 packets sugar substitute**
- **2 teaspoons vanilla**
- **2 cups sugar-free, low-fat vanilla ice cream**
- **16 blueberries**
- **4 small strawberries, halved**
- **8 peach slices**

1. Combine partially thawed strawberries, peaches, blueberries, sugar substitute and vanilla in food processor. Process until coarsely chopped.

2. Add ice cream; process until well blended.

3. Serve immediately for semi-soft texture or freeze until ready to serve. (If frozen, let stand 10 minutes to soften slightly.) Garnish each serving with 2 blueberries for "eyes," 1 strawberry half for "nose" and 1 peach slice for "smile." *Makes 8 (½-cup) servings*

Frozen Berry Ice Cream

HOT FUDGE WAFFLE SUNDAES

12 frozen mini-waffles
2 tablespoons hot fudge topping
¾ cup reduced-fat Neapolitan ice cream
4 tablespoons aerosol light whipped cream
Colored sprinkles (optional)

1. Heat waffles in toaster until lightly browned. Heat hot fudge topping in microwave according to package directions.

2. Arrange three waffles on each of four serving plates. Top with 1 tablespoon of each ice cream flavor. Evenly drizzle hot fudge topping over top; garnish with whipped cream and sprinkles, if desired.   *Makes 4 servings (3 mini-waffles each)*

COOKIE MILK SHAKES

1 pint vanilla ice cream
4 chocolate sandwich cookies or chocolate-covered
graham crackers

1. Scoop ice cream into blender fitted with metal blade. Crush cookies in resealable food storage bag with rolling pin or in food processor.

2. Place cookies in blender. Process until well combined. Pour into 2 glasses. Serve immediately.   *Makes 2 milk shakes*

Hot Fudge Waffle Sundae

SNACKIN' BANANA SPLIT

1 small ripe banana, peeled
1 small scoop low-fat or fat-free vanilla frozen yogurt
   (about 3 tablespoons)
1 small scoop low-fat or fat-free strawberry frozen yogurt
   (about 3 tablespoons)
⅓ cup sliced fresh strawberries or blueberries
2 tablespoons all-fruit strawberry fruit spread
1 teaspoon hot water
2 tablespoons low-fat granola cereal
1 maraschino cherry (optional)

1. Split banana in half lengthwise. Place in shallow bowl; top with frozen yogurt and strawberries.

2. Combine fruit spread and water in small bowl; mix well. Spoon over yogurt; sprinkle with granola. Top with cherry, if desired.

Makes 1 serving

Tip: Make as many of these easy and delicious banana splits as you may need for your ice cream party!

Snackin' Banana Split

The publisher would like to thank the companies and organizations listed below for the use of their recipes and photographs in this publication.

Del Monte Corporation

Dole Food Company, Inc.

EAGLE BRAND®

The Hershey Company

Keebler® Company

© Mars, Incorporated 2006

National Pork Board

NatraTaste® is a registered trademark of Stadt Holding Corporation

Nestlé USA

Unilever

Veg•All®

Watkins Incorporated

Beef
Kiddy Quesadillas, 24
Mini Pickle Sea Monster Burgers, 54
Taco Taters, 26
Taco Two-Zies, 22
Birthday Cake Cookies, 43
Boats in the Ocean, 52
Bride of Frankenstein Treats, 18

Cakes
Cookie Pizza Cake, 36
Dolphin Cake, 70
Happy Clown Face, 34
Lollipop Garden Bouquet, 38
Rainbow Cakes, 50
Sweet Express, The, 46
Tropical Parasol Cake, 62
Under the Sea Cake, 66

Candy
Bride of Frankenstein Treats, 18
Clown-Around Cones, 72
Dolphin Cake, 70
Fish Squishy Squirters, 64
Flying Saucer Ice Cream Sandwiches, 74
Happy Clown Face, 34
Haunted House Cupcakes, 2
Lollipop Garden Bouquet, 38
"Make Your Own Sundae" Pie, 82
Mice Creams, 84
Rainbow Cakes, 50
Squished and Squirmy Sandwiches, 80
Surprise Package Cupcakes, 44
Under the Sea Cake, 66
Caramel Sundae, 78
Cheesy Snails, 14

Chocolate (*see also* **Chocolate Chips**)
Chocolate Flan, 28
Clown-Around Cones, 72
Cookie Pizza Cake, 36

Flying Saucer Ice Cream Sandwiches, 74
"Make Your Own Sundae" Pie, 82
Peanut Butter Cup Cookie Ice Cream Pie, 76
Strawberry & Chocolate Shake, 81
Surpise Package Cupcakes, 44
Triple Chocolate Cups, 48
Under the Sea Cake, 66

Chocolate Chips
Chocolate Ice Cream Cups, 84
Dessert Nachos, 32
Ghosts at the Watering Hole, 18
Mini Morsel Ice Cream Pie, 86
Peanut Buster Bar Desserts, 87
Chocolate Flan, 28
Chocolate Ice Cream Cups, 84
Clown-Around Cones, 72
Conch Shells, 60
Cookie Milk Shakes, 90
Cookie Pizza Cake, 36
Cookie Sundae Cups, 40

Cookies
Birthday Cake Cookies, 43
Cookie Milk Shakes, 90
Cookie Pizza Cake, 36
Cookie Sundae Cups, 40
Creamy Dreamy Taco Treats, 30

Cupcakes
Haunted House Cupcakes, 2
Surprise Package Cupcakes, 44
Tropical Luau Cupcakes, 68

Dessert Nachos, 32
Dolphin Cake, 70
Dulce de Leche Dessert Sandwiches, 27
Easy Taco Pizza, 26

Fish Bait with Gator Heads, 58
Fish Biters, 56
Fish Squishy Squirters, 64

95

Flying Saucer Ice Cream Sandwiches, 74
Frozen Berry Ice Cream, 88
Fruity Dessert Cups, 86
Funny Face Fruit Pizzas, 42

Ghost on a Stick, 8
Ghosts at the Watering Hole, 18
Gushing Goo Rolls, 4

Happy Clown Face, 34
Haunted House Cupcakes, 2
Hot Fudge Waffle Sundaes, 90

Ice Cream, 72–93
Cookie Sundae Cups, 40
Creamy Dreamy Taco Treats, 30
Dulce de Leche Dessert Sandwiches, 27
Triple Chocolate Cups, 48

Kiddy Quesadillas, 24

Lollipop Garden Bouquet, 38

"Make Your Own Sundae" Pie, 82
Mice Creams, 84
Mini Morsel Ice Cream Pie, 86
Mini Nacho Pizza, 24
Mini Pickle Sea Monster Burgers, 54
Monstrous Mac & Cheese, 8

Night Crawler Veggie Rolls, 10
Nuts
Chocolate Ice Cream Cups, 84
Creamy Dreamy Taco Treats, 30
Dulce de Leche Dessert Sandwiches, 27
"Make Your Own Sundae" Pie, 82
Peanut Buster Bar Desserts, 87
Triple Chocolate Cups, 48
Peanut Buster Bar Desserts, 87

Peanut Butter Cup Cookie Ice Cream Pie, 76
Pies
"Make Your Own Sundae" Pie, 82
Mice Creams, 84
Mini Morsel Ice Cream Pie, 86
Peanut Butter Cup Cookie Ice Cream Pie, 76
Pork
Easy Taco Pizza, 26
Fish Biters, 56
Snake Calzones, 20
Putrid Bug Potion, 12

Rainbow Cakes, 50

Seafood
Fish Bait with Gator Heads, 58
Sticky Rice Coffins, 16
Snackin' Banana Split, 92
Snake Calzone, 20
Squished and Squirmy Sandwiches, 80
Sticky Rice Coffins, 16
Strawberry & Chocolate Shake, 81
Surprise Package Cupcakes, 44
Sweet Express, The , 46

Taco Taters, 26
Taco Two-Zies, 22
Tombstones, 6
Triple Chocolate Cups, 48
Tropical Luau Cupcakes, 68
Tropical Parasol Cake, 62

Under the Sea Cake, 66